I Wish, I Wish

written by
E. Elaine Watson

illustrated by
James E. Seward

© 1983, The STANDARD PUBLISHING Company, Cincinnati, Ohio
Division of STANDEX INTERNATIONAL Corporation. Printed in U.S.A.

The distinctive trade dress of this book is proprietary to Western Publishing Company, Inc., used with permission.

I wish I could have fished with Jesus.
He didn't need a pole.
He didn't need a wiggly worm.
He just said to Peter, "Put your net in the water here."
And Peter did.

John 21

Then Peter pulled the net up out of the water.
It was full of fish: lots of fish, big, big fish.
Jesus was the best fisherman.
He knew where the fish were swimming because He was Jesus.
How wonderful it must have been to fish with Jesus!   John 21

I wish I could have sat with Jesus
around the campfire:
Smelling the fish frying;
Eating the bread Jesus gave me;
Listening to Jesus talk.   John 21

Jesus asked Peter, "Do you love me?"
Peter said "Yes."
I would have said yes, too.
How wonderful it must have been to sit with Jesus around the campfire! John 21

I wish I could have walked with Jesus along the seashore:
Wiggling my toes in the sand;
Holding Jesus' hand;
Seeing Him smile at me.

I would have listened to Jesus when
 He said,
  "Love one another";
  "Be kind";
  "Give thanks to God."
How wonderful it must have been
 to walk with Jesus along the
 seashore!

I wish I could have sailed with Jesus
  in the boat:
    When the waves were splashing;
    The wind was blowing hard;
    And the boat rocked up and down,
      up and down.
But I would not have been afraid,
Because Jesus was there.   Mark 4

He told the waves to be still, and they were.
He told the wind to be calm, and it was,
Because He was Jesus.
How wonderful it must have been to sail with Jesus in the boat! Mark 4

I wish I could have climbed up the
  mountain with Jesus.
All of the people followed Him:
  The mothers and daddies,
  The boys and girls.
I would have sat next to Jesus
  In the soft grass,
  In the warm sunshine,
  And listened to Him teach the
    people,
Because He loved them.　　　John 6

I wish I could have given Jesus my lunch to feed all the people.
And watched Him break the bread and fish into pieces so everyone could eat,
Because He cared about them.
How wonderful it must have been to climb up the mountain with Jesus!

John 6

I wish I could have fished with Jesus,
Walked with Jesus,
Sat with Jesus,
Sailed with Jesus.
Climbed up the mountain with Jesus.
How wonderful it must have been!

Someday when I get to Heaven,
I want to fish with Jesus:
   Walk with Jesus;
   Sit with Jesus;
   Sail with Jesus.
How wonderful it will be!